1 Augustine's teaching on human nature

Augustine's theology gives an insight into why human nature is characterised by irrational and corrupt thoughts or actions and why God's grace is necessary. For Augustine, the Fall marks a pivotal point in human relationships, both with God and within society.

Is there a distinctive human nature?

Augustine would argue that there is a distinctive human nature because of his views on Original Sin:

- Original Sin has been inherited by all humans because they were seminally present in Adam and were all conceived through a lustful sexual act. It is like a disease that is passed on through the generations.
- There is now a permanent imbalance in human will because *cupiditas* (selfish love) is in control of *caritas* (generous love).
- The effect of this is that free will is restricted by this inbuilt nature because humans tend to make selfish and evil choices.

Others argue for a different type of human nature. For example:

- Rousseau thought that humans are essentially good and it is society that restricts them and encourages evil.
- Pelagius (a contemporary of Augustine) claimed that human nature is not flawed because sin is chosen out of free will; Original Sin is not inherited.

However, some scholars question whether there is a 'human' nature at all. For example:

- Individuals are born like a blank slate (*tabula rasa* – John Locke) and are formed by the experiences of life and upbringing.
- John-Paul Sartre argues that there is no human nature; it is up to the individual to shape their character.

Is Augustine pessimistic or optimistic about human nature?

Augustine's views of human nature and Original Sin have led to accusations of pessimism. This criticism can be justified by examining Augustine's interpretation of the Fall in Genesis 3. Augustine argued that the world was created in a state of perfection (e.g. Genesis 1:31, 'God saw everything that he had made, and it was very good') but was disrupted by the Fall.

Effects of Original Sin on:	Before the Fall	After the Fall
Human nature and will	*Caritas* and *cupiditas* were balanced and there was harmony in the human will.	Because of Original Sin, human nature was inherently corrupted, so humans can never be morally good by their own efforts.
Relationships	Adam and Eve experienced friendship, which was the highest form of relationship.	Relationships were tainted by concupiscence – uncontrolled desires such as lust, jealousy and selfishness.
Society	Society only required leaders to guide, like a shepherd.	Society is corrupted by cravings for power and wealth, so systems of law and punishment are required to keep people in order.

However, it is possible to suggest that Augustine's views of human nature are optimistic.

- Augustine is often called the 'Doctor of Grace' as his writings contain so many references to God's generous love. For Augustine, God's grace is the only cure for the illness of sin.

- God's grace is freely available to everyone because Jesus died to take the punishment for human sin.
- God's generous love is unmerited – humans can do nothing to deserve or work towards grace, they simply have to accept it.
- Then humans can achieve the *summum bonum*, an eternal, supreme goodness in the presence of God.

Is Augustine justified in his view of the Fall and Original Sin?

In reflecting on Augustine's views, try to suggest problems and counter-arguments. This will help to build a balanced evaluation in an essay. It may be helpful to create a table like the one below that lists some arguments for and against Augustine's interpretation.

Augustine's views are wrong because...	Counter-argument
His interpretation of Genesis is too literal.	A symbolic interpretation can be used instead. The Genesis myth explains why humans are sometimes evil.
The theory of evolution suggests there could not have been one couple, like Adam and Eve, that started the human race.	Adam and Eve are representative of all humans and the bad choices they make.
He was too influenced by his personal experiences of lust when he had to give up his concubine and child.	This simply highlighted the struggles against sin referred to in Romans 7 where Paul talks about doing what he does not want to do and not doing what he wants to do.
It is unfair for innocent children to be punished for the mistake of remote ancestors.	But it explains why even the youngest child makes bad choices and is not always good. Original Sin explains why humans don't deserve God's grace.

1 **Match these key terms with the correct definitions:**

Concupiscence	God's generous, undeserved and free act of love for the world, particularly seen in Jesus.
Original Sin	Uncontrolled desires and the nature of humankind being prone to sin.
Grace	Human nature is corrupt and everyone has a tendency to sin; it is inherited from Adam and passed on through the generations seminally.

2 **How and why did Augustine think that society was affected by Original Sin? Give examples and reasons in your answer.**

....

....

....

....

....

....

3 **How does this quote from Romans 7:19 support Augustine's views on human nature? 'For I do not do the good I want to do, but the evil I do not want to do – this I keep on doing.'**

....

....

....

4 Briefly outline some reasons why Augustine can be accused of having a negative view of human nature.

....

....

....

....

....

5 How and why could you argue that Augustine's view of human nature is optimistic?

....

....

....

....

....

6 Do you agree that there are characteristics which are shared by every human and inherited from birth? Why or why not? Give examples to support your view.

....

....

....

....

....

....

7 Why is the *summum bonum* important for Augustine?

....

....

....

....

....

....

8 Explain how and why the Fall and Original Sin can be interpreted symbolically.

....

....

....

9 How did the Fall affect human relationships? Give examples that illustrate these problems in relationships.

....

....

....

....

....

....

....

Exam-style question

Plan your essay here, then write the answer on a separate sheet of paper.

'Moral goodness is an impossible goal for humans.' Discuss.

AS Level – allow 35 minutes to write this essay, including 2 minutes to plan your line of reasoning.

OR: A Level – allow 40 minutes to write this essay, including 2 minutes to plan your line of reasoning.

2 Death and the afterlife

This topic covers how Christian beliefs differ about what happens in the afterlife, whether it is eternal, when judgement occurs and who will be saved.

Different interpretations of heaven, hell and purgatory

Physical places

This is the traditional view, supported by, for example:

- The Parable of the Sheep and the Goats indicates that there will be a separation at judgement to either the 'kingdom prepared for you' (Matthew 25:34) or 'eternal fire' (Matthew 25:41). This is reiterated in the Parable of the Rich Man and Lazarus (Luke 16).
- Augustine also viewed hell as a permanent, physical place of punishment ('bodies...pained by the fire', *City of God*, Book 21, Chapter 9).
- Medieval and renaissance art and literature used physical imagery, often to deter immorality (e.g. Botticelli, Michelangelo, Dante's *Divine Comedy*).
- Aquinas suggested that a purified soul is reunited with its glorified body (St Paul's version of bodily resurrection in 1 Corinthians 15) before it meets God face to face. This is referred to as the beatific vision.

A physical place for the afterlife raises several issues, including:

- the philosophical questions of identity and continuity – for example, in what sense can 'I' survive death when there is a break in continuity between my physical body left behind and a renewed body in the afterlife?
- where are heaven, hell and purgatory located?

Some argue that the idea of a physical place is a later addition to Christian theology, perhaps to provide a theological explanation for the resurrection and ascension of Jesus or to encourage moral living.

Spiritual states

- Jesus' teachings have been interpreted as referring to a spiritual kingdom of God ('Jesus answered, "My kingdom is not from this world"', John 18:36).
- Scholars such as Gregory of Nyssa and Origen see hell as a state of anguish or your conscience that tortures you with regrets and realisation of sinfulness.
- Many Catholics understand hell as a self-chosen exclusion from God; an eternal, mental state of separation.
- This solves some of the issues raised by heaven, hell and purgatory being understood as physical places. For example, if there is no need for a body in the afterlife, there is no problem of where resurrected bodies are located.
- However, there are other issues raised, for example the problem of identity – how can an immaterial soul be 'me' when so much of what makes a person unique is their physical features?
- This view also rejects the imagery of physical punishment in hell in favour of a sense of alienation from God, which may be more palatable to modern Christians.

Symbols

Some argue that heaven, hell and purgatory are symbols of moral life, which avoids the problems of an eternal afterlife. Supporting evidence includes:

- The early teaching of Jesus about the kingdom of God places more emphasis on living now rather than on a future heavenly kingdom ('The kingdom of God is within you', Luke 17:21).
- The Parable of the Sheep and the Goats emphasises the importance of actions during life, for example feeding the hungry, welcoming strangers or visiting the sick.
- The sense of reward could simply be the satisfaction, fulfilment and joy that helping others brings. Those who live selfishly or don't help others suffer from a guilty conscience and effectively torture themselves.

Who will be saved?

This is a controversial issue, so it is important to understand and weigh up the evidence from texts, scholars and sources of authority to explore the different views.

Who will be saved?	Support from texts or scholars	Problems
Limited election – only a few are chosen by God to be saved	■ The Sheep and the Goats – only those who have acted morally are saved by helping those in need, e.g. feeding the hungry. ■ Augustine said that due to Original Sin, God's grace is needed for salvation. He favoured predestination – the idea that God elected only certain people to be saved. ■ Calvin argued that only God knew who would be saved, so the elect and non-elect have a duty to act morally.	■ This seems to suggest that only good actions are needed to be saved, not faith or grace alone. ■ If Jesus dies for only a few people, his sacrifice is not effective for all, in which case why was it necessary?
Unlimited election – all are invited but only a few are saved	■ Aquinas and Catholicism teach that God elects the righteous for heaven but that the wicked select themselves for hell. ■ Karl Barth emphasised only God knows who will be saved. ■ Barth also argued that in Jesus, God is both elector and elected: Jesus is the only one who is predestined to be condemned as he died on behalf of sinful humanity.	■ Is this the same as limited election? It has a similar outcome, that only a few are saved. ■ Again, Jesus' sacrifice seems to be ineffective for everyone. ■ But this view also emphasises God's grace.
Universalism – everyone will be saved	■ Hick argues that this upholds God's love and that it seems unfair to be punished eternally for a few years of wrongdoing. In order to justify evil and suffering, everyone must eventually learn from it, develop into the likeness of God and reach heaven. ■ 1 Timothy 2:4 can be used to support the view that all can be saved: '*God...desires all to be saved.*'	■ Do humans have free choice? Could they reject salvation, or will they be saved anyway? ■ Does this mean that faith in Jesus is not necessary for salvation? This seems to make Christ's suffering and death irrelevant, which many Christians would dispute.

❶ Compare the three views about heaven and hell – as physical places, spiritual states or symbols. Which is most convincing? Give reasons and evidence to support your answer.

....

....

....

....

....

....

....

❷ Summarise the Parable of the Sheep and the Goats by answering the following questions:

a   **What do the 'sheep' do?**

....

....

b   **What happens to the 'sheep'?**

....

c What do the 'goats' fail to do?

....

....

d What happens to the 'goats'?

....

3 Why do some Christians think that heaven and hell are eternal? Give reasons to support and criticise both sides of the argument.

....

....

....

....

....

....

4 What are the different views about when judgement takes place?

....

....

....

....

....

5 Why do some Christians think that purgatory is a preparation for heaven? Why do others disagree with this view?

....

....

....

....

....

6 Why do some Christians argue that heaven is a transformation of the whole creation? Give reasons and evidence to support and criticise this view.

....

....

....

....

....

....

7 What do the following terms mean?

Limited election	....
Unlimited election	....
Universalism	....

8 To analyse and evaluate universalism, you will need to think about its strengths (supporting arguments) and its weaknesses (criticisms). Fill in this table, giving reasons *and* evidence for each view. Try to link similar or counter-arguments where you see them.

Strengths of universalism	Weaknesses of universalism
No one is condemned to hell for eternity...	It seems unfair...
God loves everyone and wants all to be saved...	What if I don't want to be saved...
Christ died so that *all* may be saved...	Why did Christ need to die...

Exam-style question

Plan your essay here, then write the answer on a separate sheet of paper.

**'Matthew 25:31–46 does not imply that heaven and hell are experienced after death.'
Discuss.**

AS Level – allow 35 minutes to write this essay, including 2 minutes to plan your
line of reasoning.

  35 · 30 marks

OR: A Level – allow 40 minutes to write this essay, including 2 minutes to plan your
line of reasoning.

  40 · 40 marks

3 Knowledge of God's existence

Questions arising in this topic include how humans can gain knowledge of God and is it possible to know about God through the world or should we rely on God revealing himself?

Natural knowledge of God's existence

Natural knowledge of God (or theology) is gained by humans reaching up to God, using reason, by observation of the world or through an inbuilt sense of the divine.

Do humans have an innate sense of the divine?

Calvin claims that humans, made in the image of God, have a 'sensus divinitatis', an inbuilt sense of and desire to know God. This is illustrated by:

- the 'seeds of religion' that are found in all cultures
- an apparent human intellectual ability to reflect on and recognise God's existence. Christian scholars such as Aquinas call 'faith seeking understanding' the principle of accommodation – God has accommodated himself to humans, allowing them to glimpse the beauty and goodness of the divine.

However, there is debate about whether Calvin rejects these forms of natural theology because:

- *sensus divinitatis* is simple knowledge superseded by revealed knowledge through the Redeemer, Jesus Christ.

Brunner argues that natural theology is limited in pointing towards God but salvation requires revelation through Jesus.

Barth, meanwhile, thinks Calvin totally rejected natural theology. Barth says that *sensus divinitatis* comes after a person has responded to God's grace through faith, so revealed knowledge of God is more important.

How can God be known through creation?

- Calvin sees creation as God's theatre, as it is like a stage revealing God's goodness.
- In Romans 1, Paul refers to the knowledge of God that is available to everyone through the natural world.
- 'The heavens declare the glory of God' (Psalm 19:1) expresses the awe and wonder we often feel when looking at creation.
- Observation of the natural world is used in teleological arguments, which focus on the purpose, order and design in nature to infer God's existence (e.g. Paley's analogy of the watch and the eye, Aquinas' Fifth Way, Tennant's anthropic principle).
- Brunner calls these 'points of contact' between God and humans, or 'sparks of glory' that help us to engage with and begin to know God.

Issues raised by natural knowledge of God

- Natural theology is accused of being too vague – it only leads to knowing *about* God, or what he might be like.
- Barth argues that human reason is so corrupt due to the Fall that natural knowledge of God is impossible. He argues that because of this, Calvin rejected natural knowledge of God.
- However, Brunner disagrees with Barth's views on Calvin's theology. Brunner argues that humans are not corrupt on a spiritual level so can access God through reason and conscience.

Revealed knowledge of God's existence

Revealed knowledge of God (or theology) is more about God revealing himself through faith, grace and the person of Jesus Christ, as portrayed in the Bible and/or the Church. Some argue revealed knowledge leads to knowing God personally, much like in a relationship.

Knowledge through faith and God's grace

- God reveals himself in the gift of grace to an individual, who then responds with faith.
- For Aquinas, knowing God through faith means making an intellectual decision to believe.
- For Calvin, it is a more emotional experience. Faith is given by God, through the Holy Spirit, who helps those who are willing to believe.

Knowledge of God in Jesus Christ

- Calvin recognised that 'simple' or natural knowledge of God was limited and that salvation requires revealed knowledge through Jesus, the Redeemer. Jesus is the 'Mediator' bridging the gap between God and humans, allowing reconciliation and full knowledge of God.
- Calvin also referred to Jesus as a 'mirror' revealing the heart of God to the world through his teachings and actions. These are recorded in the Bible and in Church tradition.
- The life of the Church continues to reveal knowledge of God through its liturgy and community projects, for example.

Is faith enough?

- If God is infinite and 'radically other', as Barth suggests, humans are too corrupt or finite to know God through natural theology. God would need to reveal knowledge which humans access through faith alone.
- Barth's emphasis on the importance of faith led him to suggest that *sensus divinitatis* comes only after a person has responded to God's grace through faith.
- However, faith by itself could lead to irrational or dangerous beliefs. Aquinas argues for 'faith seeking understanding' and the use of reason alongside faith.
- Many Christians value natural theology as a first step towards knowing God or as a confirmation that faith is reasonable.
- Both Calvin and the Catholic Church emphasise that faith alone (fideism) is not enough – God's grace is also needed.

---

1 **Is human nature too corrupt to be able to know God? Discuss and analyse different views, providing reasons for each.**

....

....

....

....

....

....

....

....

....

....

2 **Make a list of some evidence for Brunner's view that there are points of contact between God and humans.**

....

....

....

....

....

3 In what ways can knowledge of God be revealed through Jesus Christ?

....

....

....

....

....

....

4 Outline three strengths of revealed knowledge of God. After each one, add a counter-argument that highlights a weakness.

Strength of revealed knowledge of God	Counter-argument or weakness

5 Assess the opposing views in the Barth–Brunner debate about Calvin's theology. Whose arguments are more convincing? Give reasons for your view.

....

....

....

....

....

....

6 **a** Make a bullet-point list of how knowledge of God could be revealed through the life of the Church.

....

....

....

....

b To what extent do you agree? Weigh up and give reasons for your conclusion.

....

....

....

....

....

....

....

7 Are revealed and natural knowledge of God the same thing? Make a list of arguments that you could use in an essay.

....

....

....

....

....

....

....

....

8 'We can only know God if we have faith.' Outline some arguments that agree and disagree with this statement.

....

....

....

....

....

....

....

Plan your essay here, then write the answer on a separate sheet of paper.

Critically compare the arguments for natural and revealed knowledge of God.

AS Level – allow 35 minutes to write this essay, including 2 minutes to plan your line of reasoning.

 35 **30 marks**

OR: A Level – allow 40 minutes to write this essay, including 2 minutes to plan your line of reasoning.

40 **40 marks**

4 The person of Jesus Christ

This focuses on questions about who Jesus was and the main aims of his teachings and actions. It is important to analyse the set texts (and any other relevant texts you have studied), reflect on different interpretations and think about the issues raised.

Son of God

Jesus' relationship with God has been much debated. Was it special or unique, human or divine? And did Jesus himself think he was divine?

There is some evidence that suggests Jesus is divine.

- Jesus seemed to have a unique relationship with God, for example he used the intimate term 'Abba' (Dad) to address God.
- Jesus performed miracles such as walking on water (Mark 6:47–52) and healing the blind man (John 9:1–41). Jesus' resurrection from the dead is used as evidence that he is the Son of God.

However, others claim that Jesus was not divine but merely displayed a special relationship with God that all can aspire to imitate.

- Jesus had special insights or knowledge of God which he shared with his followers, for example he taught them to pray using 'Abba' and 'Father' to address God.
- Jesus showed by example how humans could live focused on God's ways, for example: 'love God…and love your neighbour' (Luke 10:27).

There is also debate about the sayings of Jesus in the Gospels. For example, during the healing of the blind man, Jesus says, 'I am the light of the world' (John 9:5):

- The use of the unspoken name of God, 'I am', could indicate Jesus thought he was divine.
- However, this wording could be a later addition by an editor of the Gospel of John because they wanted to emphasise Christian beliefs that Jesus was the divine Son of God.

Teacher of wisdom

Jesus' moral teachings seem to follow a wisdom tradition found in the Old Testament. This genre is paralleled in Jesus' succinct sayings about how to live (see the Sermon on the Mount, Matthew 5–7) and his memorable parables.

Jesus' teaching on repentance and forgiveness

Make sure you have read the Parable of the Lost Son (Luke 15:11–32) and focus on how and why it illustrates repentance and forgiveness. For example, consider the following:

- The son's actions would have been shocking at the time because he was effectively wishing his father had died.
- The extravagant forgiveness of the father envisages a more loving and less judgemental God, contrasting with the unforgiving elder brother with whom many in Jesus' audience would have sympathised.
- Genuine repentance seems to be a realisation and admission of wrongdoing and a conscious decision to take a new direction. The parable gives reassurance that those who repent will be forgiven.

Jesus' teaching on inner purity and moral motivation

- The Sermon on the Mount (Matthew 5:17–48) can be used to show that Jesus is more concerned with internal motives than with outward appearances, unlike the Pharisees and teachers of the law.
- Jesus talks about keeping the law, avoiding anger, adultery, divorce, vows, revenge and loving enemies.
- This is challenging teaching to put into practice. For example, Jesus says even looking at someone with lust or in anger is as bad as committing adultery or murder.

Liberator

Key texts like the healing of the bleeding woman (Mark 5:24–34) and the Parable of the Good Samaritan (Luke 10:25–37) help us to investigate how far Jesus challenged the political and religious authorities. These texts raise a key question about Jesus' role: was his main mission to start a political revolution or was he more concerned with liberating the poor and marginalised from the injustices of religion or society? Some possible starting points for reflection are as follows:

- Jesus reaches out to the marginalised by singling out the religiously unclean woman in a crowd. This challenges the religious traditions and authorities.
- The 'Good Samaritan' would normally be ostracised from the religious community because of his mixed-race heritage, yet Jesus uses him as a hero to challenge religious and social stereotypes.
- Jesus suffered crucifixion, the punishment of a political criminal and revolutionary at the time. Perhaps this indicates he *was* a political revolutionary but his mission ultimately failed.
- Some argue that Jesus' message of political revolution has been purposely hidden, edited out of the Gospels to make Christianity less of a threat to the Roman state.

Was Jesus 'only a wise, moral teacher' or 'more than a political liberator'?

Although this question allows for some comparison with another part of Jesus' ministry, it is not asking for everything you know on this topic. The bulk of your answer should focus on the specified aspect, i.e. 'wisdom teacher' or 'political liberator'. Consider the extent to which Jesus fits the description by reflecting on the strength or weakness of the evidence.

1 Did Jesus think he was divine? Fill in the table with reasons and evidence to support both sides of the debate.

Yes – Jesus thought he was divine because:	No – Jesus did not think he was divine because:

2 What issues are raised by claims that Jesus Christ is the Son of God?

3 Why do some claim that Jesus was fully human? Give reasons and examples to support this view.

....

....

....

....

4 What does Jesus teach about:

a Repentance?

....

....

b Forgiveness?

....

....

5 Why were Jesus' teachings on moral motivation so radical and challenging? Give examples in your answer.

....

....

....

....

....

6 Give reasons why some think Jesus was only a wise, moral teacher.

....

....

....

7 a Give reasons why some think Jesus was a political liberator.

....

....

....

....

b   Give reasons why some disagree that Jesus was a political liberator.

....

....

....

....

8 Why do some understand Jesus to be a religious liberator?

....

....

....

....

9 Which viewpoint do you find more convincing – that Jesus was a wise teacher, a liberator or the Son of God? Give reasons for your view.

....

....

....

....

....

....

....

....

Exam-style question

Plan your essay here, then write the answer on a separate sheet of paper.

'Jesus' relationship with God was so unique that it is of no help to Christians today.' Discuss.

AS Level – allow 35 minutes to write this essay, including 2 minutes to plan your line of reasoning.

35 · 30 marks

OR: A Level – allow 40 minutes to write this essay, including 2 minutes to plan your line of reasoning.

40 · 40 marks

5 Christian moral principles

This topic will reflect on the strengths and weaknesses of the different ways Christians make moral decisions. For example, some Christians may use:

- the Bible alone (based on theonomous ethics, God is the source of authority)
- the Bible alongside the Church and reason (based on heteronomous ethics, with many authoritative sources)
- only the principle of love (based on autonomous ethics, the individual has authority).

Is the Bible a comprehensive moral guide?

- In theonomous ethics, God's will is the source of all morality, which in practice leads to Christians using the Bible as a complete moral guide and the only authority on ethics.
- This works well for those Christians who read the text literally, considering it to be God's words directly given to the authors to write down. The Bible has the authority of law and is treated like a book of rules to be obeyed, so there is no need to use reason to work out what to do in each situation.
- However, there are issues when it comes to using a literal interpretation of the Bible as a moral guide. How would a Christian choose between contradictory guidelines in the Bible (perhaps between the Old and New Testaments) or decide about modern issues, such as euthanasia, which are not specifically mentioned in the Bible?
- One solution could be using reason, as in heteronomous ethics. If the Bible represents the authors' own experiences of God which they were inspired to record, it contains advice on how to live a godly life rather than being a comprehensive rule book.

Are Christian ethics personal or communal?

- Personal interpretations of the Bible or using it as the sole source of authority could lead to errors and misunderstanding, so many Christians prefer heteronomous ethics.
- The Catholic Church focuses on how the Bible has been interpreted and continues to be used in the living tradition of the Church, as well as applying reason to make ethical decisions.
- Although some Protestants emphasise individual responsibility, many will also use communal gatherings such as preaching in church services and group Bible study to help them decide how to act.
- Some argue that Jesus' ethical teaching was communal and intended to build a radical new community whose members acted together to challenge society's values.
- However, this shift of responsibility to church leaders could discourage personal faith or allow abuses of power within the Church.
- Yet you could argue that autonomous ethics better reflect Jesus' emphasis on *agape* (love) because there is greater flexibility to respond to each unique circumstance.

Is the principle of love enough to live a good life?

This question is asking whether morality should be based *only* on love and whether this provides enough guidance to make ethical decisions. Consider the following points as a starting point for discussion:

- Jesus' teaching on *agape*, particularly the Golden Rule ('Do unto others as you would have them do to you', Matthew 7:12), is the foundation of all his practical teaching. Jesus leads by example in serving the poor, weak and marginalised as well as in his own self-sacrifice.
- Following the principle of love avoids creating a list of rules that must be followed and may be outdated. Instead, each decision depends on the individual and the situation, using their human reason and so making it easier to apply *agape* to the challenges of today's world.
- However, there are also weaknesses to prioritising love because it may allow excuses for immoral behaviour or be too difficult to practise. Also, some rules are necessary to provide guidelines and even Jesus' teaching originates from Old Testament law, which he showed how to fulfil.

Are Christian ethics distinctive?

To answer this question, reflect on the similarities and differences between Christian and other religious or secular ethical systems.

- Similarities can be found between the laws of the Bible and those of the state. Teachings on the value or sanctity of life also underpin international human rights laws.
- Most religions are founded on a principle of concern for others or unselfishness to which Christians have simply added a unique label, *agape*.
- Nevertheless, the principle of *agape* is more radical and challenging in Christianity because it includes self-sacrifice.
- You could explore the extent to which Jesus' teachings provide a unique moral model. For example, Gandhi promoted non-violent protest rather than revenge, while Jesus asked his followers to 'love your enemies'.

1 **Compare the three types of Christian ethics. Fill in the table to help you remember the differences.**

	Theonomous ethics	Heteronomous ethics	Autonomous ethics
What does it mean?			
How do Christians decide what is moral?			
Give an example of how it helps with moral decisions.			

2 **Why do some Christians think the Bible is the most important source of authority?**

3 What are the strengths and weaknesses of using a combination of the Bible, Church and reason to work out ethical principles?

....

....

....

....

4 Why do some argue that reason must be used to understand the Bible?

....

....

5 Should Christian moral principles be decided by the individual alone? Give reasons for different views.

Yes:

....

....

....

....

No:

....

....

....

....

6 a   Why does the Catholic Church argue that Christian ethics must be communal? Give reasons.

....

....

....

b   What are the problems with this view?

....

....

....

....

7 Why is the principle of *agape* a useful tool for Christian ethical decision-making? Give reasons.

....

....

....

8 Do you think Christian ethics are distinctive?

- Give reasons for and against.
- Weigh up (evaluate) which side is stronger.
- Write a final sentence which explains why you have come to this conclusion.

....

....

....

....

....

....

....

....

Exam-style question

Plan your essay here, then write the answer on a separate sheet of paper.

To what extent should Christians rely solely on the Bible for deciding moral principles or actions?

AS Level – allow 35 minutes to write this essay, including 2 minutes to plan your line of reasoning.

 30 marks

OR: A Level – allow 40 minutes to write this essay, including 2 minutes to plan your line of reasoning.

 40 marks

6 Christian moral action

This section focuses on the teachings and example of Dietrich Bonhoeffer. Bonhoeffer's theology was influenced by his experiences in Nazi Germany during the Second World War. He encouraged Christians to act on the teachings of Jesus and not to remain silent or do nothing in the face of suffering and evil.

Should Christians practise civil disobedience?

Bonhoeffer advocated using civil disobedience for several reasons:

- It is more important for a Christian to obey God than to obey human leaders. Christians should hold the state accountable using God's laws.
- Also, if the state is asking its citizens to 'do the unreasonable', Christians have a duty to withdraw their support.
- If Christians remain silent, they are condoning the evil, so they should speak and act for the voiceless.
- Christians should address the causes of injustice by putting a 'spoke in the wheel' rather than simply bandaging the injured.

Biblical texts can be used to support or criticise Bonhoeffer's view. For example:

- Jesus supported the political system by paying taxes ('give to Caesar what is Caesar's and to God what is God's', Matthew 22:21).
- St Paul stated that kings and rulers were given authority by God to govern, so Christians should not promote disorder in society (Romans 13:1–7).
- However, in the Bible prophets spoke out against injustices when the rulers were failing (e.g. Amos 5:11–15).
- Jesus helped the marginalised and challenged the status quo (e.g. Mark 5:24–34, Luke 10:25–37).

Is it possible to know God's will?

Bonhoeffer justified his actions in disobeying state laws and even plotting tyrannicide by claiming to do the will of God. However, how can Christians be sure they are doing God's will, particularly if the action goes against traditional moral principles? Is Bonhoeffer giving Christians an excuse for extremism or terrorism?

Bonhoeffer's response included:

- Human nature is sinful and our judgement of what is right or wrong is affected too.
- All humans can do is to act out of despair with faith and hope. God's will would 'only be clear in the moment of action'.
- Although he recognised some actions are sinful, such as tyrannicide, he thought God promised to forgive 'the man who becomes a sinner in the process'.

The Church as a community

Bonhoeffer was involved in the Confessing Church founded by the Barmen Declaration of 1934 but later became disillusioned with its lack of action against Hitler. Bonhoeffer's views of what the Church should be like included:

- For Christians:
  - The Church should be a supportive and challenging community. For example, the seminary at Finkenwalde encouraged its members to live a disciplined physical and spiritual life, with daily exercise, prayer and Bible study.
  - The community of believers were accountable to each other. This could help with working out the will of God, or challenging eccentric interpretations of texts.
- For those outside of the Church:
  - The Church should exist for others just as Jesus was a 'man for others'.
  - He thought that the Church should be outward looking – as salt and light in the world (Matthew 5:13–16).

Why does Bonhoeffer emphasise suffering?

- Bonhoeffer argued that following Jesus is difficult. God saves Christians by grace, which cost God his son and cost Jesus his life. Christian disciples should also be willing to give up everything, even their own life, and should expect sacrifice and suffering. Bonhoeffer described this as 'costly grace'.
- True discipleship contrasts with 'cheap grace', which refers to those who accept Jesus' sacrifice for their sins but do not change their lives. This cheapens Jesus' suffering.
- Bonhoeffer thought Christians should stand in solidarity with the marginalised and voiceless, such as the Jews who were being persecuted in Nazi Germany. This also led to Bonhoeffer suffering with them.

Is Bonhoeffer's theology relevant today?

Yes	No
The Gospel message is the same – following Christ should be whole-hearted, putting God's will and others before ourselves.	This seems outdated in our secular, post-modern era when individual rights are the most important consideration.
Christians continue to have solidarity with those on the margins of society and can draw attention to injustices.	Christians should keep their religion in churches. It is the job of the government or charity organisations to look after the poor.
Minorities (including Christians) continue to be oppressed and persecuted by some regimes.	Bonhoeffer lived in extreme times so his solutions are not relevant today.
Civil disobedience can lead to peaceful change, for example the civil rights movement in the USA.	Modern democracies replace the need for civil disobedience. We can vote for political leaders to change society.

1 **Fill in the definitions for the specialist vocabulary:**

Religionless Christianity	
Civil disobedience	
Tyrannicide	

2 **'We are not to simply bandage the victims under the wheels of injustice, but we are to drive a spoke into the wheel itself.' Explain this quote from Bonhoeffer. Do you agree with his view?**

3 Should duty to God come above duty to the state? Give reasons for your view.

....
....
....
....
....

4 Give reasons for and against the view that Christians should be involved in civil disobedience.

....
....
....
....
....
....
....
....

5 Why did Bonhoeffer become disillusioned with the Confessing Church? Was he right? Why or why not?

....
....
....
....
....
....

6 Why was the community at Finkenwalde important to Bonhoeffer?

....
....
....

7 What are the strengths and weaknesses of Bonhoeffer's teaching about suffering?

....
....

....
....
....

8 Explain the difference between 'costly grace' and 'cheap grace'.

....
....
....

9 How did Bonhoeffer put his teaching on solidarity into practice?

....
....
....
....

Exam-style question

Plan your essay here, then write the answer on a separate sheet of paper.

Critically examine Bonhoeffer's approach to Christian discipleship.

AS Level – allow 35 minutes to write this essay, including 2 minutes to plan your line of reasoning.

 30 marks

OR: A Level – allow 40 minutes to write this essay, including 2 minutes to plan your line of reasoning.

 40 marks

7 Religious pluralism

This section is concerned with how Christian theology engages with the contemporary multi-faith context. Issues include the response to other religions, whether Christians should try to convert those of other faiths or none, and how Christians can promote dialogue and social cohesion.

Religious pluralism and theology

Does theological pluralism undermine central Christian beliefs?

This question arises from the claims of pluralism that all religions lead to God and that belief in Jesus is not necessary for salvation. Different approaches to these issues can be broadly divided into pluralism, inclusivism and exclusivism.

- Pluralism – Hick argued that all religions are valid interpretations of the divine; each leads to salvation in its own way. This does not undermine central Christian beliefs, but it fulfils the essence of Christianity because it emphasises the benevolence of God. Jesus is a role model for sacrificial selflessness.
- Inclusivism – Rahner argued against pluralism because it undermined the importance of Christ's death and resurrection. Inclusivism understands Christianity to be the usual way to salvation, but that God's grace may be seen in other religions. Those who seek God through other religions are 'anonymous Christians'.
- Exclusivism – Calvin argued for *solus Christus* (salvation through Christ alone) because Jesus said, 'I am the way, the truth and the life, no one comes to the Father but by me' (John 14:6). The role of Jesus is essential and is what makes Christianity distinctive.

Will all good people be saved?

This question is asking whether faith in Jesus is needed for salvation or whether it is enough to live a moral life, with or without religion. Christian responses vary, for example:

- Exclusivism may argue that salvation requires faith. This can be supported by texts such as Titus 3:5: 'He saved us, not because of works done by us in righteousness, but according to his own mercy.'
- Inclusivism may allow for good people to be saved if they are anonymous Christians. Perhaps they have not heard the Christian message yet and so respond to God through actions rather than belief.
- Pluralism may argue that there are good people in all religions and since each religion contains some element of truth, this must be enough for salvation. Also, a loving God would allow everyone to be saved.

Religious pluralism and society

Multi-faith societies

Multi-faith societies have developed for many reasons, including migration and globalisation. The UK has encouraged migration at various times, for example from the West Indies after the Second World War; from India and Pakistan in the 1960s. This has led to diverse faiths being practised and a sharing of values and festivals, for example. Advances in technology have enabled increased communication, trade, travel and the spread of ideas. Multi-faith societies provide opportunities and challenges for Christians.

Christian mission

Redemptoris Missio 55–57 and *Sharing the Gospel of Salvation* tackle the issues of being a Christian in a multi-faith society, including whether the Christian mission to 'make disciples', or convert others, is still relevant today. Think about the similarities and differences in the approach of these two documents.

- Both emphasise that mission and inter-faith dialogue are equally important for all Christians.
- Both recognise that although God can reveal himself through other religions, full salvation is available only through Christ.
- *Redemptoris Missio* emphasises the need for conversion and baptism into the Church, whereas *Sharing the Gospel of Salvation* focuses on openness, respect and loving one's neighbour through community projects and social justice as well.

Has inter-faith dialogue helped social cohesion?

Some arguments that inter-faith dialogue has helped social cohesion include:

- It promotes tolerance, working together for the common good and an appreciation of shared values, for example through joint community projects or worship.
- It can help to give a voice to those on the margins of society.

Some possible counter-arguments are:

- The practical outcomes of inter-faith dialogue are difficult to measure but its purpose is to explore faith, not social cohesion.
- It has been ineffective and causes more divisions because some religious people reject inter-faith dialogue.
- As secularisation increases, fewer people are influenced by religion, so inter-faith dialogue becomes redundant.
- The lack of social cohesion could be a symptom of social problems and injustice, which need to be addressed first, for example poor housing, social inequality and poverty.

The Scriptural Reasoning movement

The Scriptural Reasoning movement started in the 1990s with representatives from Judaism, Christianity and Islam but is now open to all religions. The Cambridge Inter-faith Programme is one example of how Scriptural Reasoning has been used in inter-faith dialogue. Scriptural Reasoning aims to build trust and appreciation of shared beliefs and values by discussing interpretations of a religious text.

Think about whether this helps or hinders religious belief. Some suggestions are included in the table.

Scriptural Reasoning helps religious belief	Scriptural Reasoning challenges religious belief
Believers can explore religious texts from different perspectives, which can revitalise their own understanding.	If there are conflicting opinions, how do you know which is true?
There is a greater appreciation of the texts and traditions of others, which promotes tolerance.	It could cause conflicts with your own beliefs or tradition.
It encourages shared values.	It might lead to less religious distinctiveness.

1 Fill in the table with strengths and weaknesses of exclusivism.

Strengths	Weaknesses

2 Is faith in Jesus necessary for salvation? How and why would each of the following approaches answer this question?

a Exclusivism.

    b   Inclusivism.

    ....

    ....

    ....

    c   Pluralism.

    ....

    ....

    ....

3 Why do some Christians find inclusivism convincing?

....

....

....

....

4 Is Christianity distinctive or just the same as all other religions? Give reasons for each view.

....

....

....

....

....

....

....

5 Does being good guarantee salvation? Give reasons for and against your view.

....

....

....

....

....

....

6 Evaluate whether the advantages of Scriptural Reasoning outweigh the disadvantages.

....

....

....

....

....

....

7. Is it more important for Christians to share their faith or to help those in their community? Give reasons for your view.

....

....

....

....

....

....

8. Compare *Redemptoris Missio* and *Sharing the Gospel of Salvation* by filling in the table:

What do they say about...?	*Redemptoris Missio*	*Sharing the Gospel of Salvation*
The centrality of Christ		
Mission and converting others		
Inter-faith dialogue		

9 Is *Redemptoris Missio* or *Sharing the Gospel of Salvation* more useful for Christians today? Give reasons for your view.

....

....

....

....

....

....

Exam-style question

Plan your essay here, then write the answer on a separate sheet of paper.

Critically assess whether Christians should try to convert those who do not have a faith.

Allow 40 minutes to write this essay, including 2 minutes to plan your line of reasoning. (40) (40 marks)

8 Gender

The issues raised in this section revolve around whether secular views of gender and gender roles should affect Christian teaching or practice. The challenges of feminism to Christianity are discussed in relation to the theology of Mary Daly and Rosemary Radford Ruether.

Gender and society

The idea of family

- Catholics and some Protestants argue that the biblical pattern of family is based on heterosexual marriage. For example, Ephesians 5:22–33 states, 'Wives submit to your husbands...the husband is the head of the wife.' Traditionally this has meant that the wife is subservient to her husband as Christ is head of the Church.
- However, other Christians have suggested that the main message of these household rules is about mutual love and relationships which are Christ-like. The writers were influenced by the values and tradition of their times, so the important message for Christians today is the principles of family life, especially the centrality of love and respect, rather than a specific type of family.
- This view could also be supported by those who argue that the idea of family is culturally determined rather than being determined by a religious ideal. For example, even the Bible portrays a variety of family or household types which reflect the norms of its society (e.g. Jacob's extended family, Genesis 46; polygamous marriages, 1 Kings 11; baptisms of whole households, Acts 16:14–15).

Motherhood

Mulieris Dignitatem 18–19 presents a Catholic view that understands motherhood as a privilege for women, which gives them a special status similar to that of Mary, the mother of Jesus. It suggests that women and men have complementary gender characteristics. Women have biological and psychological instincts for child-rearing, and although shared parenthood is recognised, men should acknowledge that it is more demanding for the mother.

- This could help liberate women because it releases them to fulfil a special purpose and appreciates the sacrifices they make for their children.
- However, others may suggest this is patronising because it tries to make the subservience of women more palatable.
- Feminists such as Simone de Beauvoir argue that motherhood restricts women by confining them to the home and preventing them from developing a full career.
- Some feminists would challenge the idea of innate gender characteristics, suggesting these are not innate but constructed by society. In this case, motherhood should be a choice for women rather than an expectation.

Gender and theology

Gender terms and God

- In the radical feminism of Mary Daly, *Be-ing* replaces God as a spiritual process of the continual discovery of the richness of nature. She argues that gender-neutral terms should be adopted.
- Rosemary Radford Ruether explores goddess language because she argues that patriarchal overtones should be removed to make the divine accessible to women. She also emphasises the importance of using the Old Testament female wisdom principle, *Sophia*, in describing the Christian God rather than the male term *Logos*.
- The Catholic Church states that God transcends gender, so perhaps Christians need to move away from using gender terminology.
- However, some Christians may prefer to resist the influence of feminism and continue to use traditional, male-orientated language.

Should Christianity be changed or abandoned?

- In reflecting on the challenges presented by secular feminism and modern ideas of gender, Christians need to consider whether to resist this influence, to welcome reform or even to abandon outdated practices altogether.
- *Mulieris Dignitatem* suggests that the Church should resist secular gender influences. It emphasises the equality of women and men in their different roles in the family and in society. It should be the Church that provides a model of how mutual respect can enhance the separate roles of women and men.

Radford Ruether on the maleness of the Church

Rosemary Radford Ruether argues for reform of Christianity from within the Church.

- She argues that the Church needs to return to the authentic message of Jesus by rejecting the androcentric editing of biblical texts.
- For example, she claims the masculine idea of Jesus as a warrior-Messiah has hidden the authentic, liberating wisdom tradition. Jesus' actions challenged the unjust treatment of the marginalised and were counter-cultural in his treatment of women.
- Jesus ignored patriarchal gender roles and established a community of equals based on faith. Radford Ruether supports the Women-Church movement as a way of rediscovering this egalitarian ideal.

Daly on sexism in Christianity

The radical feminist theologian Mary Daly argues for the abandonment of Christianity because it is outdated and irrelevant for women. Daly claims that sexism within Christianity has serious implications:

- Christianity is entrenched in patriarchy, illustrated by its 'Unholy Trinity' of rape, genocide and war.
  - Rape refers to the oppression of women, often through violence but also metaphorically, for example in pornography and through the virgin birth of Jesus.
  - Genocide results from a rape culture in which one group dominates and destroys another group (e.g. Joshua 11). It also includes the destruction of the natural world.
  - War is a symbol of male values; the Church advocates 'Just War' yet will not allow abortion or euthanasia.
- The biblical text was written by men, for men and promotes masculine ideals which glory in the mistreatment of women.
- 'If God is male then the male is God' – Daly argues that the centrality of Jesus Christ has led to the male becoming God, so women continue to be subservient to male leaders in the Church. This is seen in the Catholic Church in particular where only men can be priests.
- Daly suggests Christianity should be abandoned in favour of a spirituality based in nature, with which women have a particular affinity.

---

1 **'Men and women are equal but different.' How can this be used to explain Christian beliefs about gender roles?**

....

....

....

....

....

....

....

2 Read Ephesians 5:22–33.

a   How can it be used to support the ideas of a traditional Christian family?

....

....

....

....

b   How can it be used to challenge the ideas of a traditional Christian family?

....

....

....

....

3 Why does the Catholic Church argue that motherhood is liberating? Use sources of authority to support your reasoning, such as *Mulieris Dignitatem*.

....

....

....

....

....

4 Why do some people argue that motherhood is restricting? Give reasons, using scholars' views to support your answer.

....

....

....

....

....

5 Is the idea of family determined by culture? Give examples and reasons to support your view.

....

....

....

....

....

6 Should Christians resist secular ideas on gender? Give reasons for and against and include examples.

....

....

....

....

....

7 Compare the feminist theology of Rosemary Radford Ruether and Mary Daly. Use the table to help you compare similarities and differences.

	Radford Ruether	Mary Daly
Should Christianity be reformed or abandoned? Why?		
How important is nature in spirituality?		
What is the role of women in Christianity?		

8 Why does Radford Ruether argue that the female wisdom principle is important?

....

....

....

....

9 **What does Mary Daly mean by Christianity's Unholy Trinity?**

....

....

....

....

....

....

....

Exam-style question

Plan your essay here, then write the answer on a separate sheet of paper.

Critically compare the approaches of Daly and Radford Ruether to the idea of a male saviour.

Allow 40 minutes to write this essay, including 2 minutes to plan your line of reasoning. **40** **40 marks**

9 The challenge of secularism

Secularism could challenge Christianity because it seeks to keep religion and state separate, perhaps by limiting religion to private life. Secularisation goes further and aims to remove religious influence from public institutions such as government and education.

Freud and Dawkins

Freud's views can be used to support secularism as he argues that religion should be abandoned. One reason is that the desire for a father figure is a psychological construct which helps make sense of the trauma of the natural world and death. In Christianity, this wish fulfilment is projected onto God.

Dawkins also considered that society would be better without religion, for example because he claims that scientific enquiry has made religion obsolete by explaining issues such as 'how the world began'. However, Stephen J Gould disputes this, arguing that science and religion belong to different but equal categories. John Polkinghorne suggests both science and religion are needed to give a full explanation of the human experience.

Are spiritual and human values the same?

Consider some similarities and differences between Christian and secular values.

- Universal morals reflect a common human bond and they are not unique to religion.
- Humanism argues that reason can work out principles for moral living. The 2002 Amsterdam Declaration of the World Humanist Congress contains shared values, for example:

Humanist values	Christian values
Respect for democracy and human rights	Do not steal others' property; have a non-working day in the week
Dignity of all humans	Do not kill
Personal liberty should be combined with social responsibility	Jesus and the Church have promoted liberation of the poor and social justice
Valuing artistic creativity	Christianity has been the source of a large tradition of art and literature in the Western world

- Although Christian tradition has often promoted the use of reason, it points to a divine origin for moral commands, which gives them further authority. Christian ethics are radical and distinctive, shown in the teaching of Jesus. For example, the command to love your enemies is counter-cultural because the natural human reaction is often revenge.

Does Christianity cause social and personal problems?

Christianity causes social and personal problems	Counter-arguments
Freud claims that religion is an obsessional neurosis caused by repressed guilt which resurfaces as psychological problems such as compulsive behaviour.	Religion can provide meaning, purpose and fulfilment. Religion also gives answers to some of the complex questions we ask, such as 'Why are we here?'
Dawkins points to examples such as the Crusades to argue that religion is dangerous; it causes conflicts within and between societies.	Christians are sinful humans and so should acknowledge and ask forgiveness for mistakes of the past. However, Christians make positive contributions to society, for example food banks, inter-faith dialogue and social justice campaigns.
Christianity causes conflict with liberal, modern society because it holds on to outdated beliefs, for example about the sanctity of life and sexuality.	Some Christians would argue that there are universal values that need to be upheld and that some things are always right or wrong. Society needs to be reminded, for example, of the value of each individual.

Christian responses to secularism

Some Christians embrace secularism because:

- it challenges Christians to become more relevant in the modern world
- it provides an opportunity for Christians to contribute to society at every level, by promoting equality and a voice for all citizens.

However, some Christians choose to reject secularism and secularisation because:

- they are dangerous and don't recognise the strength of feeling religion evokes. Some argue that religious fanaticism has arisen as a reaction to secularism.

Should Christianity have a role in public life?

Yes	No
Christianity is part of the history and traditions of the UK and so should remain part of public life, such as in politics and education.	Humanism argues that governments should be completely separate from religious organisations and that all groups should be treated equally.
It provides checks against immoral laws, for example the bishops in the House of Lords can veto or amend laws.	Reason and conscience can be used by all politicians so there is no need for religion to be represented in government.
Faith schools are useful in society because they help diversity and integration.	Faith schools should be closed because they segregate society and can be a breeding ground for radicalisation.

1 What is the difference between secularism and secularisation? Give a definition and example for each.

2 What reasons does Freud give for his claim that God is an illusion?

3 Why does Dawkins argue that society would be better off without religion? Give reasons to justify his view.

....

....

4 Outline the role of Christianity in:

   a   **Education and schools.**

....

....

....

   b   **Government and state.**

....

....

....

5 Weigh up the strengths and weaknesses of politics and religion being separate in public life.

....

....

....

....

....

....

....

6 Make a list of examples of common values that are shared by all humans and those that are distinctly Christian.

Examples of shared human values	Examples of distinctly Christian values
....	....
....	....
....	....

7 To what extent are all values common to humanity? Use the table from Question 6 to weigh up reasons for your answer.

....

....

....

....

....

....

8 How and why can secularism provide opportunities for Christianity?

....

....

....

....

....

....

Exam-style question

Plan your essay here, then write the answer on a separate sheet of paper.

Evaluate whether Christianity is irrelevant to modern society.

Allow 40 minutes to write this essay, including 2 minutes to plan your line of reasoning. 40 marks

10 Liberation theology and Marx

There are several ways that liberation theology has used and been influenced by Marxism, for example:

- Liberation theologians have adopted the Marxist tool of 'praxis' to analyse the causes of poverty and then to act to change society.
- Both systems reject using the patterns of alienation, which dehumanise people and prevent them from living fulfilling lives.
- Both challenge the injustices of capitalism, which can be a cause of exploitation when people are treated as objects and 'a means to an end'. This can result in corruption, which gives wealth to the rich at the expense of the poor.
- Marxism has been used to refocus theology from abstract principles to the daily struggles of ordinary people.
- Liberation theology also challenges the Church to use its wealth and power more effectively to tackle issues of poverty and inequality.

Although the influence of Marxism can be traced in liberation theology, some people argue that liberation theology's roots are found in the Bible. Liberation theologians use the hermeneutic of suspicion to ask questions of and to reinterpret texts, for example:

- The Exodus is a journey from slavery to freedom.
- The prophets challenged the corruption of the rich and injustices against the poor.
- Jesus' ministry was for those on the margins of society who were exploited or rejected.
- Jesus taught about the kingdom of God as a reversal where the last will be first and the meek inherit the earth. An equal society is envisaged.

Christianity and atheist ideologies

Has liberation theology been too influenced by Marxism? Should Christian theology engage with secular, atheist ideologies? Arguments to consider include:

- Marxism understands the Church to be part of the problem, acting like an 'opiate' to dull the effects of oppression with promises of an afterlife. Some ask how Christians can engage with an atheist ideology that wants to destroy it.
- Others reject Marxism because communism, its associated political system, has been unsuccessful in establishing a more just society.
- Some liberation theologians have also adopted Marxist ideas of revolution, not ruling out violence to achieve justice in society. Others disagree with this – for example, the Catholic Church has distanced itself from Marxism and emphasises the need to alleviate spiritual (rather than material) poverty.

Addressing social issues

Is Marxism or liberation theology more effective in tackling social issues? Some differing views to understand include:

- Marxism may be more effective because it argues that the whole structure of society needs to be revolutionised first. Only then will wealth be shared equally and the oppressed be free.
- Liberation theology challenges the wider Church and its acceptance of capitalist and materialist values. It can work from within the Church to bring change. However, some argue that reform is too slow and ineffective.
- Some liberation theologians (e.g. Gustavo Gutierrez) focus initially on the sin built into the structures of society, such as corruption and exploitation, followed by challenging the sin of individuals. However, others, such as Juan Segundo, argue that Christianity mainly liberates individuals from personal sinfulness; this is more important than trying to change society.
- The spiritual aspect of life, criticised by Marxism, can be a source of great strength and transformation. Christians can respond on a more local and personal level to the needs of the community and practise sacrificial love, perhaps by identifying and living alongside the poor.

Should Christians give priority to the poor?

Liberation theology argues for a 'preferential option for the poor', which means giving priority to the poor, marginalised and oppressed. Use what you know about Jesus' teaching and actions, particularly as a liberator, and examples from the Bible to assess whether this is the heart of the Christian message. Further ideas to consider include:

- The 'kingdom of God' incorporates the idea of reversal, a bottom-up theology, rather than imposed doctrine from the church hierarchy above. For example, 'the last shall be first' (Mark 10:31).
- It is more important to feed the hungry, give a drink to the thirsty, or help the sick and those in prison (Parable of the Sheep and the Goats, Matthew 25:31–46) than to teach them Christian doctrine. Right action, or orthopraxis, should be prioritised by helping the poor before teaching them Christian beliefs.
- Some, such as Pope Benedict XVI, disagree and argue that orthodoxy, or official Christian teaching, is paramount. It is the distinctive, spiritual message of Jesus which should be preached and which will lead to changed lives.

---

1 **Write out the definitions for the following technical terms:**

Alienation	
Praxis	
Orthopraxis	
Orthodoxy	

2 **How and why does Marx criticise religion and other aspects of society?**

....
....
....
....
....
....
....

3 **Should Christians be involved in violent means to change society? Why or why not? Use examples from liberation theology to support your view.**

....
....
....
....

4 What is a hermeneutic of suspicion? How has it been used by liberation theology? Give examples.

5 Is liberation theology right to prioritise orthopraxis over orthodoxy? Give reasons for your view, showing you have considered counter-arguments.

6 How can Jesus' teaching about reversal in the kingdom of God be used to support liberation theology?

7 Should Christians give priority to one group over another? Give reasons for and against this view.

8 To what extent does individual sin need to be tackled before social sin? Compare the arguments and write a conclusion.

....

....

....

....

....

....

....

Exam-style question

Plan your essay here, then write the answer on a separate sheet of paper.

'Christian theology is in a direct but fruitful confrontation with Marxism.' Discuss.

Allow 40 minutes to write this essay, including 2 minutes to plan your line of reasoning.

Hachette UK's policy is to use papers that are natural, renewable and recyclable products and made from wood grown in well-managed forests and other controlled sources. The logging and manufacturing processes are expected to conform to the environmental regulations of the country of origin.

Orders: please contact Hachette UK Distribution, Hely Hutchinson Centre, Milton Road, Didcot, Oxfordshire, OX11 7HH. Telephone: +44 (0)1235 827827. Email education@hachette.co.uk Lines are open from 9 a.m. to 5 p.m., Monday to Friday. You can also order through our website: www.hoddereducation.co.uk

ISBN: 978 1 5104 4933 6

© Karen Dean 2019

First published in 2019 by
Hodder Education,
An Hachette UK Company
Carmelite House
50 Victoria Embankment
London EC4Y 0DZ

www.hoddereducation.co.uk

Impression number   10 9 8 7 6 5 4 3

Year   2023 2022 2021

Cover photo © MIGUEL GARCIA SAAVED - stock.adobe.com

Typeset in India

Printed in the UK

A catalogue record for this title is available from the British Library.

HODDER EDUCATION

t: 01235 827827
e: education@hachette.co.uk
w: hoddereducation.co.uk

ISBN 978-1-5104-4933-6

MIX
Paper from
responsible sources
FSC™ C104740